George Frederic Heydt

Charles L. Tiffany and the house of Tiffany & Co

George Frederic Heydt

Charles L. Tiffany and the house of Tiffany & Co

ISBN/EAN: 9783337150907

Printed in Europe, USA, Canada, Australia, Japan

Cover: Foto ©Andreas Hilbeck / pixelio.de

More available books at **www.hansebooks.com**

CHARLES L. TIFFANY
and the House of
TIFFANY & CO.

TIFFANY & CO.
Union Square, New-York.
1893.

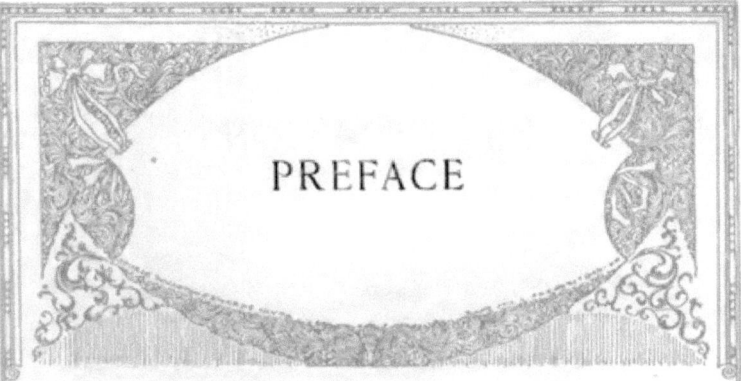

PREFACE

In this brief sketch of Mr. Charles L. Tiffany, and of the house which he founded and still directs, the days of earlier New-York, for half a century past, are briefly traced, and events in the history of the nation are incidentally noted.

The house of Tiffany & Co. occupies a unique position in its relation to the development of the fine arts and beautiful creations of our nation and century. The inseparable ties that associate it with the growth of the country, and the interest manifested in its early history and in the various stages of its career, are such that the following pages have been written in deference to the wish of many old friends and patrons of the house for an authentic review.

The writer hopes that he has gathered from an extensive mass of material many things of sufficient interest to reward the reader for the time spent in the perusal of these pages.

GEORGE FREDERIC HEYDT.

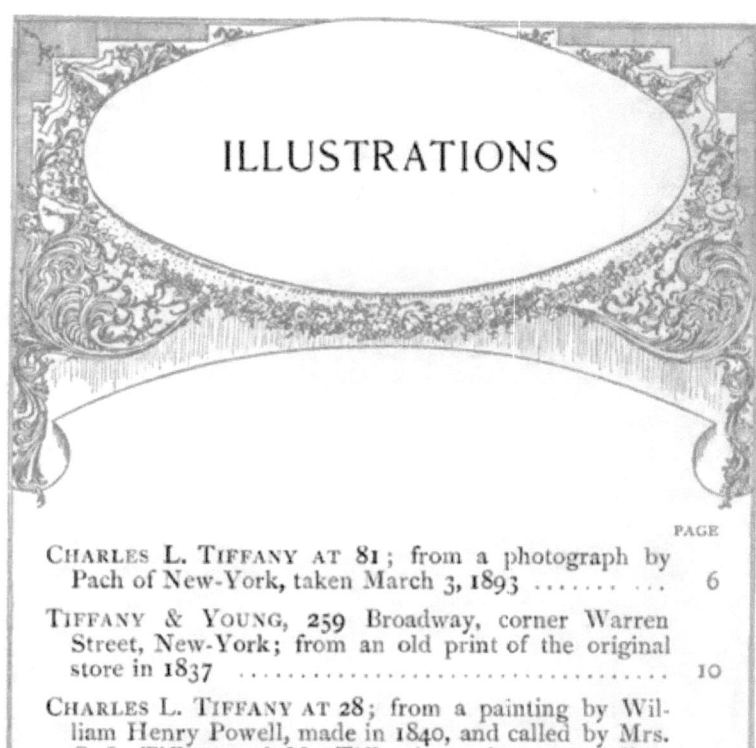

ILLUSTRATIONS

Genealogy. CHARLES LEWIS TIFFANY, founder of the house of Tiffany & Co., is a descendant, in the sixth generation, of Squire Humphrey Tiffany of England. His great-great-grandfather, great-grandfather, and grandfather were natives of Massachusetts. Squire Humphrey Tiffany, the original ancestor, was killed by a stroke of lightning on July 15, 1685, while on the road to Boston. Comfort Tiffany, the father of Charles L. Tiffany, was born in Attleboro, Mass., and, after marrying Chloe Draper, daughter of Isaac Draper of that town, he removed to Danielsonville, Windham County, Conn., where he embarked in the manufacture of cotton goods.

Comfort Tiffany established his home on the Killingly side of the Quinebaug River, and here on February 15, 1812, Charles L. Tiffany, the eldest son, was born.

Early School=Days. THE boy was brought up in the town of his birth, and received his primary education in the "little red schoolhouse" at Danielsonville,—a typical New England district school,—and later spent two years at the Plainfield (Conn.) Academy, about ten miles from his home. This was at that time a noted educational institute, presided over by John Witter, a graduate and tutor of Yale.

While young Tiffany was at the Plainfield Academy, his father, Comfort Tiffany, who had already been engaged in the manufacture of cotton goods in Danielsonville for about twenty years, formed a new company for the same purpose. They bought half of the water privilege of the Quinebaug River, on the Brooklyn side, and began operations under the name of the "Brooklyn Manufacturing Co." While building the new mill, Comfort Tiffany opened a little country store, and gave his son Charles, then but fifteen years old, full charge; and in this inconspicuous way Charles L. Tiffany made his *entrée* into the commercial world. He kept the books of the store, and when the business had become firmly established he made frequent trips to New-York for supplies.

About a year after the opening of the new mill, Comfort Tiffany established his home over on the Brooklyn side of Danielsonville, and some time later bought out the interests of his other partners in the "Brooklyn Manufacturing Co.," and operated the plant under the name of "C. Tiffany & Son." After the business of the little country store had developed, and the elder Tiffany had erected a more commodious store for its purposes, the additional help required afforded young Charles L. an opportunity to take up his studies again, and with several short terms at the Brooklyn school he finally finished his education.

1837 - 1847. THE year 1837 was the turning-point in his life. From the little Connecticut village he ventured out into the maelstrom of metropolitan life. New-York was then a city of over 200,000 inhabitants, and proportionately as crowded with business enterprises as it is to-day. Young Tiffany's business venture was not an accident,—it was born of a deliberate purpose, the result of his conclusion that the future of the cotton industry in Connecticut offered nothing to satisfy his ambition. Hence he determined to seek a wider field of activity.

His neighbor, friend, and schoolmate, John B. Young, had gone to New-York six months before him, and was employed in a stationery and fancy-goods store. Mr. Tiffany followed early in September of 1837. New-York was then in the throes of perhaps the greatest commercial crisis of its history. Many well-established concerns were on the verge of ruin. Mr. Tiffany's ambition, however, was not to be daunted by this grave state of affairs. He and his former schoolmate went carefully over the field together, and concluded to unite Mr. Young's limited stock of experience with whatever capital could be advanced by Mr. Tiffany's father, and to open a fancy-goods and stationery store. The elder Tiffany being appealed to, he consented to loan the young men a thousand dollars, $500 to be assumed by each partner.

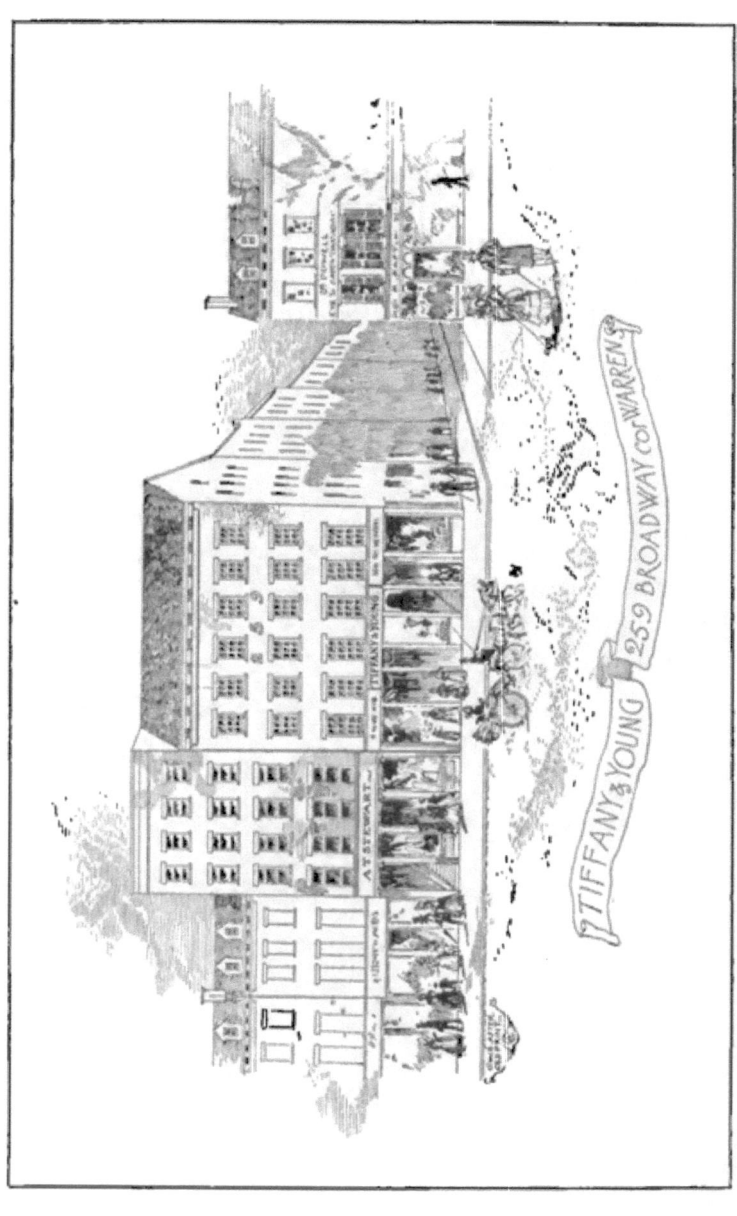

HISTORY
OF
THE HOUSE

Tiffany & Young. THE young men entered into a partnership under the firm-name of "Tiffany & Young," and thus was laid the foundation of the present house of Tiffany & Co. The difficulties which they encountered in finding a desirable location which should come within their limited means, in running the chances of success without any knowledge of metropolitan business methods, in starting out in the very face of the worst commercial depression in the history of the country at that time—these and other obstacles, which to most men would have seemed insurmountable, were overcome by this young firm in a manner that augured well for their future success.

A suitable site for their first venture was finally found in an old-fashioned double dwelling-house at 259 Broadway. Half of the lower part was already occupied by Mme. N. Scheltema, a fashionable modiste; the other half, with a frontage of fifteen feet, was obtainable at a moderate rental; the only serious objection urged against the premises being that they were too far up-town. Marquand & Co., the leading jewelers of those days, were located at 181 Broadway, near Cortlandt Street, and within a few blocks of them were clustered all the jewelers and dealers in high-class fancy articles who had any prominence at that time.

11

It was A. T. Stewart who perhaps unconsciously turned the balance in favor of No. 259. Mr. Stewart, already a successful merchant of ten years' standing, had his own store next door to Mme. Scheltema's, and belief in the sagacity of the future dry-goods king led the young men to decide upon this up-town location. This perplexing question disposed of, there followed the problem of how to open business with a stock sufficiently unique and choice to attract custom to a new house.

One of Mr. Tiffany's most noted traits, and one that has distinguished the house in its entire career, is an instinctive avoidance of beaten paths. He was ever devising original methods and seeking unique objects. The store was stocked with salable merchandise. Choice and novel objects in bric-à-brac; Chinese goods, then very popular; Japanese *papier-mâché* and terra-cotta wares; umbrellas, walking-sticks, desks, dressing-cases, cabinets, fans, fine stationery, pottery, fancy articles, and curiosities of every description,— these things soon became marked features of the store of Tiffany & Young.

First Cash-Book. THE little store was opened to the public on the morning of September 18, 1837. The total sales for the first three days amounted to only $4.98; with this they opened their first cash-book. The next day $2.77 was added. But the high character of the stock soon became generally known; patronage increased, and new features were added. On the day preceding Christmas of the same year, the sales footed up $236, and on New Year's Eve the receipts amounted to $675. New Year's Day, according to old Knickerbocker usage, was then the approved occasion for the interchange of gifts, as Christmas is now.

The following year marked a steady though uneventful growth; but on the morning of January 1, 1839, the young firm was robbed of nearly all it possessed. The thieves, who carried away almost everything portable of value, had also evidently calculated upon appropriating the largest single week's receipts of the year; but luckily the two partners had taken the precaution to empty the cash-drawer and carry the contents home with them.

Their loss amounted to nearly $4000; but they quickly recovered themselves, and the business continued to prosper to such an extent that early in 1841 it was found necessary to rent the adjoining corner store, No. 260. This gave them a frontage of forty-five feet on Broadway and a window running down on Warren street. With the increased space at their disposal, the scope of the business was rapidly enlarged. Bohemian glassware, French and Dresden porcelain, cutlery, clocks, and fancy Parisian jewelry were added in the order named.

Tiffany, Young & Ellis.

THE year 1841 was in more respects than one a memorable one in the history of the young firm. The first important step during the spring of the year was the admittance of another partner, Mr. J. L. Ellis; the firm-name becoming "Tiffany, Young & Ellis."

The business had now grown to such proportions that the disadvantages of importing stock without a thorough personal knowledge of what the European markets afforded were daily growing more evident. After the addition to the firm, it was decided that one of the members should go abroad in search of novelties for their exclusive trade. This method of Mr. Tiffany's for obtaining choice selections for retailing at first hand was a unique one fifty years ago. Mr. Young was selected to make the trip, and being well supplied with letters of introduction from prominent personages, he had an *entrée* to all the leading European houses.

He returned home with the choicest examples of the novelties to be found abroad.

Mr. Tiffany's Marriage. THIS year of successes also marked the happiest turning-point in Mr. Tiffany's career. Just before the holidays he took another step the wisdom of which has been proved by over fifty years of uninterrupted domestic happiness. On November 30, 1841, he was married to Miss Harriet Olivia Avery Young, sister of his partner, and daughter of Judge Ebenezer Young of Killingly, Connecticut. This union brought them six children. Four are living and reside, some in the house of their parents, others in homes of their own, near by. Charles Lewis, Jr., the first-born, died at the age of four, and Henry Charles, the third child, died at the age of one. Mr. Tiffany's family now consists of his wife, Mrs. Charles L. Tiffany, and children, Annie Olivia (Mrs. Alfred Mitchell), Louis Comfort, Louise Harriet, and Burnett Young Tiffany.

Manufacture of Jewelry. REVERTING to Mr. Tiffany's business career, the success of the first journey abroad warranted annual visits to the European markets, and led to the introduction of useful and fancy articles of a higher order of taste, beauty, and richness than had ever been seen before in New-York. The house had now established for itself a reputation which made it the resort of all who were in search of rich and costly articles of luxury. Shortly the cheap grades of jewelry from France, Hanau and Frankfort, Germany, gave way to a better quality of English jewelry, and this in turn was followed by Italian or Roman jewelry. During this time the mosaic

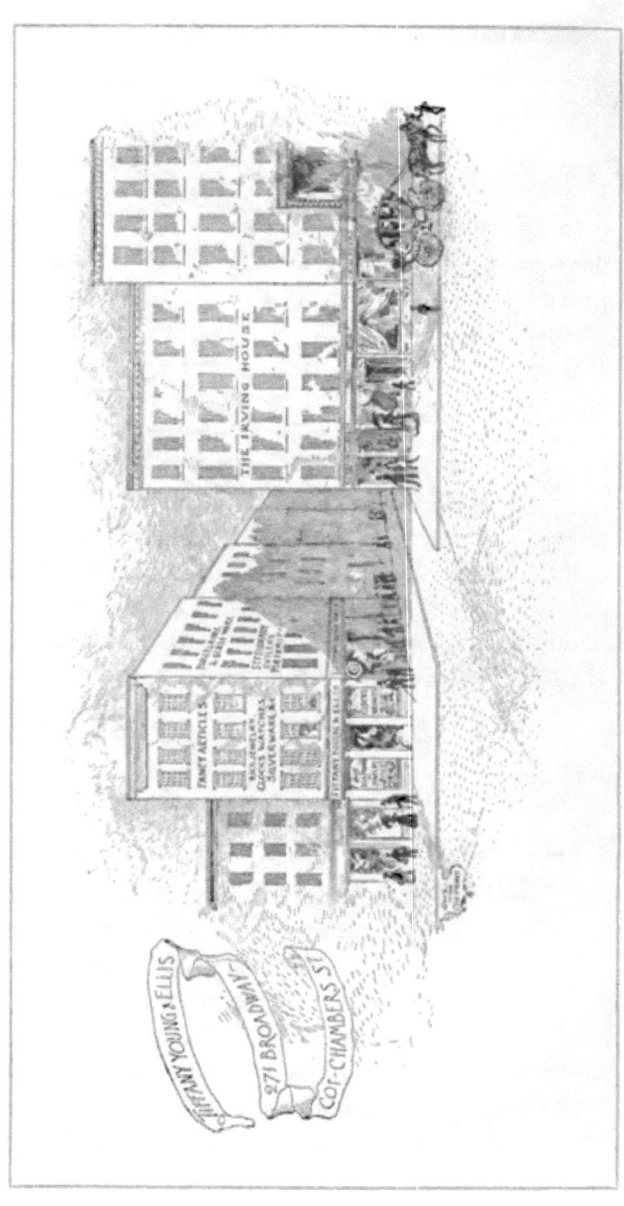

work from Florence and Rome, and the finer jewelry from Paris, enjoyed a period of popular favor running over many years. Gradually, however, American jewelry encroached upon the field to such a degree that when in 1848 the firm began the manufacture of gold jewelry, it quickly became one of the most important branches of their business.

No. 271 Broadway.

BEFORE the close of the first ten years the continued increase necessitated another removal, which took place in 1847. A much larger and more modern store was secured at 271 Broadway, corner of Chambers Street, and the business rapidly expanded in every direction. Diamond jewelry, watches, clocks, silverware, and bronzes became the leading features of a stock which had now grown so complete in articles of luxury that the house issued an annual catalogue for the convenience of their patrons.

The Revolution of 1848.

THE political disturbances of 1848 in Paris afforded many opportunities for shrewd investments. In the panic that followed, diamonds declined about fifty per cent. Mr. Tiffany and his partner, Mr. J. B. Young, were quick to grasp the situation, and immediately decided to invest all the available resources of the firm in these precious gems. Mr. Young, accompanied by Mr. Thomas Crane Banks, who conducted the jewelry department for the house, had just arrived in Paris, prepared to make large purchases of jewelry and European novelties; but instead of searching for the latter, they directed their whole attention and resources to the purchase of diamonds. In spite of suffering arrest as suspects, and encountering numerous other unpleasant experiences in the panic-stricken city, they yet fulfilled their mission so successfully as to raise the firm of Tiffany, Young & Ellis to the front rank of diamond merchants.

Historic Gems.

THIS first large purchase of gems was followed by many others. Notable among these were the investments in historic gems, of which Tiffany & Co. have probably been among the largest purchasers in the world.

Among the most famous gems which passed into their possession was the zone of diamonds worn by the ill-starred Marie Antoinette. This zone was bought by the house in Paris about forty years ago. At the great sale of diamonds of the famous Hungarian Prince Esterhazy, some years later, Tiffany & Co.'s purchases amounted to over $100,000. But the largest investment ever made by them in historic gems was in 1887. At the sale of the crown jewels by the French government, Tiffany & Co. purchased 24 lots of the stones—over one third of the entire amount—at a cost of 2,285,700 francs (about $500,000): a larger amount than the total purchases of the nine next largest buyers.

Paris Branch, 1850.

IN 1850 Mr. Gideon F. T. Reed, formerly of Lincoln, Reed & Co., the leading jewelers of Boston, was admitted into partnership. Immediately after, the first branch house was established at 79 Rue Richelieu, Paris, Mr. Reed becoming the resident partner in Paris, where the house was conducted under the firm-name of Tiffany, Reed & Co. This branch house proved an invaluable acquisition to the firm, Mr. Reed's residence abroad enabling him to take advantage of all the fluctuations in the European markets.

Like the New-York house, the Paris branch developed rapidly. From the little office in Rue Richelieu, it removed to 57 Rue du Cardinal Fesch, afterward named Rue de Châteaudun. At the present time it occupies very spacious quarters at Avenue de l'Opéra 36 bis. Since the retirement of the late Mr. Reed, the foreign branch has been continued under the name of Tiffany & Co. Americans resident or traveling abroad have for many years largely patronized the Paris house, and to-day the stock to be seen there includes the choicest features of the Union Square establishment.

Sterling Silver. ONE of the first innovations made by Tiffany & Co. was that of using the highest practical grade of silver in all their productions. Up to this time, old Spanish and Mexican coins contributed largely to the supply of metal used; but in these coins there was no uniformity of standard.

Tiffany & Co. introduced the English standard of sterling silver—$\frac{925}{1000}$ fine. Their example was immediately followed by all the other leading silversmiths of that period, and the standard, which Great Britain found necessary to protect with a "hall mark," soon became established in this country upon the reputation of an individual firm. What the house has since accomplished in developing American art in metal-work is matter of history. At the Paris Exposition in 1867 Tiffany & Co.'s productions won for American silverware the first award of merit from a foreign jury, and at the International Expositions of 1878 and 1889 the firm received the Grand Prix and a special decoration of the Legion of Honor. The honors bestowed upon the house at the Centennial Exhibition of 1876, and the World's Columbian Exposition of 1893, are touched upon elsewhere.

Manufacture of Silverware.

WHEN the late P. T. Barnum brought Jenny Lind to this country in 1850, one of the first shops visited by the famous singer was Tiffany's. Mr. Tiffany recalls with pleasure the first order he executed for her. It was a costly silver tankard, made for presentation to the captain of the ship which had brought her over. This testimonial—one of the first silver pieces of note made by the firm—was a masterpiece of ideas which, even in these days of advanced art, it would be difficult to excel. Its decorations were thoroughly nautical, from the graceful handle—a mermaid rising out of a billowy sea—to the Triton emerging from the cover. Part of the decoration on the tankard represented a rainbow, which marked an incident of the trip which the famous singer desired to remember.

The improvement in the manufacture of silverware, both in form and decoration, had by this time (1851) become recognized, and with the recognition came rapidly increasing demands for special presentation pieces and household articles. The productions of John C. Moore, who made silverware for Marquand & Co., and also for their successors, Ball, Tompkins & Black, were then attracting considerable attention for their solidity and artistic conception. Mr. Tiffany observed in the general character of Mr. Moore's work a strength and individuality wholly different from those of any other manufacturer. It was the quality he had always sought for, and his discovery proved of mutual advantage, for an arrangement was made with Mr. Moore whereby the latter was to manufacture solely for Tiffany & Co.

Upon the retirement of the elder Mr. Moore, he was succeeded by his son, the late Edward C. Moore, who had learned the trade in his father's factory. The skill he had acquired under the tuition of his father, with the resources of Tiffany & Co. and their rapidly growing business, developed the little shop with its handful of employees into an industry of extraordinary proportions, covering to-day almost

TIFFANY & CO.'S JEWELLERY STORE, 550 BROADWAY, NEW YORK, AS IT APPEARED IN THE ILLUMI-
NATION DURING THE TELEGRAPHIC JUBILEE, SEPTEMBER 1, 1858.

of the chastest specimens of architecture in Broadway, was ready-made clothing for wholesale a

an entire block in Prince Street, and giving employment to a force of about 500 men.

Tiffany & Co., 550 Broadway.

THE year 1853 marked another important change in the composition of the firm. On May 1, Messrs. J. B. Young and J. L. Ellis retired, and with the admission of new partners the business was from that day continued under the present firm-name of Tiffany & Co. The change resulted in materially broadening the scope of the business, and the continued increase of the business made another removal necessary in 1854. A new building was erected for their accommodation at No. 550 Broadway, between Spring and Prince streets. This location was then considered so far above the business territory of Broadway, that many questioned the wisdom of the change.

The firm took possession of their new quarters on May 1, 1854, and before long the former critics of Mr. Tiffany commended him for his keen foresight. The firm remained upon this site for sixteen years, the most eventful of their existence, marked by an immense growth in their business, and by many historic incidents. In 1861 they added the adjoining building, No. 552 Broadway, which afforded facilities for meeting the pressure of business incidental to the war, and otherwise enlarging their field of activity.

Atlantic Cable.

UPON completion of the first great Atlantic cable in 1858, Mr. Tiffany made a clever stroke by purchasing the remaining cable, many miles in all, and cutting it up into souvenirs of the event, making paper-weights, cane, umbrella, and whip handles, bracelets, seals and other watch-charms, festoons, and coils for ornamenting parlors and offices. When the articles were put on sale, policemen were required to maintain order among the crowds who were eager to buy the souvenirs. The following advertisement from "Frank Leslie's Weekly" of September 11, 1858, may be of interest:

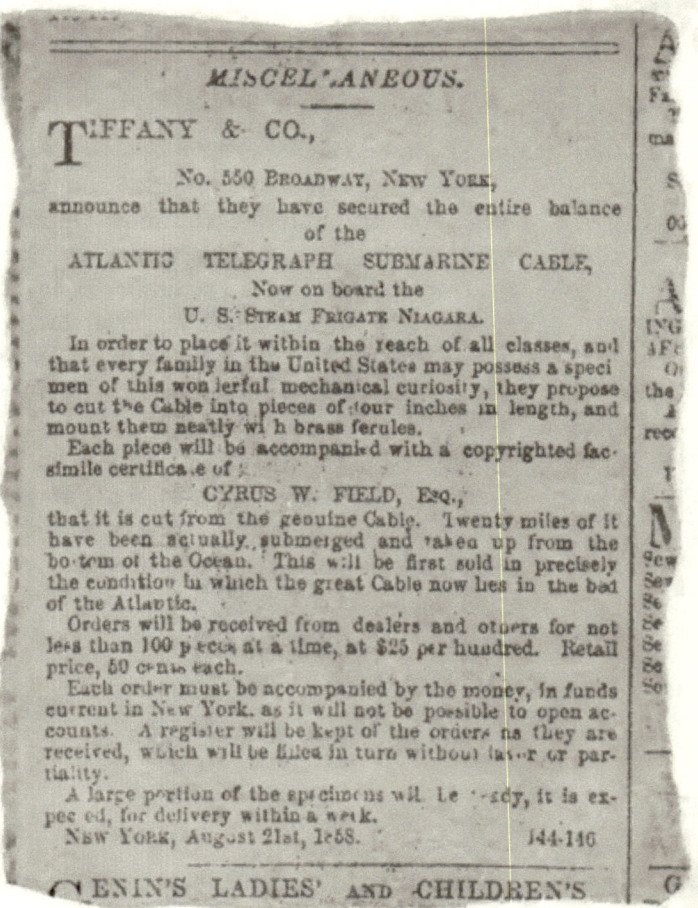

MISCELLANEOUS.

TIFFANY & CO.,

No. 550 Broadway, New York,
announce that they have secured the entire balance
of the
ATLANTIC TELEGRAPH SUBMARINE CABLE,
Now on board the
U. S. Steam Frigate Niagara.

In order to place it within the reach of all classes, and that every family in the United States may possess a specimen of this wonderful mechanical curiosity, they propose to cut the Cable into pieces of four inches in length, and mount them neatly with brass ferules.

Each piece will be accompanied with a copyrighted fac-simile certificate of

CYRUS W. FIELD, Esq.,
that it is cut from the genuine Cable. Twenty miles of it have been actually submerged and taken up from the bottom of the Ocean. This will be first sold in precisely the condition in which the great Cable now lies in the bed of the Atlantic.

Orders will be received from dealers and others for not less than 100 pieces at a time, at $25 per hundred. Retail price, 50 cents each.

Each order must be accompanied by the money, in funds current in New York, as it will not be possible to open accounts. A register will be kept of the orders as they are received, which will be filled in turn without favor or partiality.

A large portion of the specimens will be ready, it is expected, for delivery within a week.
New York, August 21st, 1858.   J44-146

GENIN'S LADIES' AND CHILDREN'S

Civil War, 1861 = 64.
BETWEEN the period of the first Atlantic Cable Jubilee in 1858 and the celebration in 1866 of its final success, came the Civil War. While others, uncertain as to what attitude they

should assume, were wavering in their duty, Mr. Tiffany's patriotism and prudence once more asserted themselves. Foreseeing a prolonged struggle, he promptly made arrangement with his partners to devote the capital and facilities of the house to the support of the Government.

He was the first to submit to the Quartermaster-General a complete model of the equipments of the French army. The elegant show-rooms where the arts that wait on peace and plenty had formerly held full sway, were transformed into a depot for military supplies.

Orders for all manner of supplies came in from all over the country — French rifles, ambulances and army shoes, cavalry, army and navy swords and equipments of every kind. Twenty thousand badges were made for the State of Ohio alone, while non-commissioned officers' swords, caps, rifles, army shoes, medals, and corps badges were manufactured and shipped by thousands. A commentary upon the thoughts uppermost in men's minds in those days of '61 is found in the following gruesome advertisement reproduced from the war files of "Frank Leslie's Weekly":

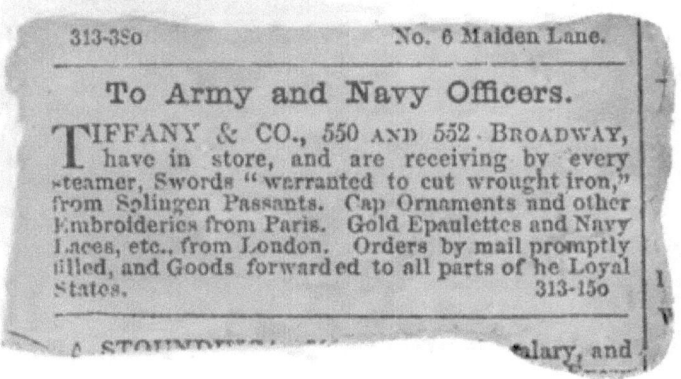

During the draft riots in 1863, when the mob was moving down Broadway and word came that they were intent upon storming Tiffany & Co.'s store and other business houses,

Mr. Tiffany barricaded the doors of his store, filled bombs, and charged hand-grenades himself, and with his employees stood ready to defend the firm's property. Fortunately, however, the army of rioters did not get beyond Bleecker Street before they were headed off by the police.

Paris Exposition, 1867. SOON after the Atlantic Cable Jubilee in 1866, Tiffany & Co. again became conspicuous,—this time at the Paris Exposition of 1867. They wisely made no attempt to rival the productions of old-established houses abroad, or the elaborate masterpieces of European art, but confined themselves almost exclusively to a display of the plainer patterns of domestic plate. The grace and beauty of these designs, together with their delicacy of workmanship and solidity of construction, called forth the encomiums of the European press, and resulted in the house receiving the first award ever offered to a foreigner. In commenting upon the above, the London "Spectator" said: " We confess we were surprised and ashamed to find at the Paris Exposition that a New-York firm, Tiffany & Co., had beaten the Old Country and the Old World in domestic silver-plate."

The reputation established by Tiffany & Co. during the war for promptly executing great orders, as well as the laurels won at the Paris Exposition for the superiority of their productions, gave the firm an impetus which placed them in the front rank of the world's jewelers. Their store, already one of the largest of its kind, was once more inadequate for their business.

Incorporation, 1868. THE firm was incorporated as a manufacturing company under the laws of the State of New-York in 1868, with Mr. Tiffany as president and treasurer; Gideon F. T. Reed, vice-president; Charles T. Cook, general superintendent and assistant treasurer; and George McClure, secretary. Upon Mr. Reed's retirement in 1875 from active participation in the management of the business, Mr. Charles T. Cook succeeded him as vice-president.

Mr. Cook's connection with the house of which he is now the vice president dates back to 1848, and the circumstances which led to his employment were not in any essential particulars different from the surroundings that daily mark the experiences of thousands of others entering upon a business career.

Since the incorporation of the business he has shared with Mr. Tiffany the responsibility of its general management. Mr. Cook's work has brought him in touch with most of Tiffany & Co.'s patrons during the last twenty-five years; and to his executive abilities, and the judgment which he exercised, Mr. Tiffany attributes much of the success that has come to the house.

The incorporation of the house as a manufacturing company was followed by a general expansion of the business, including the manufacture of watches, clocks, etc. The silverworks in Prince Street were united to the commercial department and considerably enlarged, and then Mr. Edward C. Moore became a director in the company and manager of its manufacturing interest.

London Branch, 1868. At about the same time a branch house was established in London, England, with an office at 29 Argyll Street; but soon more spacious quarters were needed, and a removal was made to 5 Argyll Place. At present the London house occupies a handsome store at 221 and 221A Regent Street, where a large assortment of Tiffany & Co.'s productions are always kept in stock.

The establishment of the London branch was followed

by the construction of a large plant for the manufacture of
watches in Geneva. This was the largest factory ever
erected in Switzerland for that purpose. Arrangements
were made to unite the best European skill with the latest
mechanical improvements and labor-saving methods that
American ingenuity could devise. It was a unique experi-
ment, and to it the house directed the lavish resources and
energies at its command.

The first Geneva office was established in 1868 at 7 Rue
Leverrier, and a salesroom for watches, jewelry, and diamonds was opened a few years later at 10 Grand Quai,
pending the completion of their watch-factory. This was
erected at the Place Cornavin — where it still stands — in
1872, but after a thorough trial the conditions surrounding
European labor were found to be wholly inapplicable to
American methods. Better results were obtainable by turn-
ing both patterns and patents over to a watch-company to
operate and manufacture the superior timepieces required
by the firm.

Union Square, 1870.

As an immediate result of the
incorporation, steps were taken
to provide more adequate quarters for the business, which
had entirely outgrown the facilities of 550 and 552 Broadway.

Upon the corner of Union Square and 15th Street, the
present site of Tiffany & Co.'s establishment, stood Dr.
Cheever's ivy-covered "Church of the Puritans," which
during the war became famous through Dr. Cheever's
fierce onslaughts upon slavery.

The church had just been vacated, and the property, with
a frontage of 78 feet on Broadway and 140 feet on 15th Street,
was offered to Tiffany & Co. The picturesque Square and
other advantages led to a quick decision, although the conditions of sale necessitated the purchase of the church with
all its fittings, including organ, pews, etc. Plans were im-

Tiffany & Co.,
Union Square, New-York.

mediately drawn for an absolutely fire-proof building; and
the present five-story structure was one of the first strictly
fire-proof buildings erected in the city.

The building was completed late in the fall of 1870, and
on November 10th formal possession was taken. The old
Spingler House adjoined the new store, while all around
the Square were mostly private residences, nor was a business house within sight on West 14th Street. It was origi-
nally designed that the second and third floors should be
rented out; but before desirable tenants could be found
the business had increased so rapidly that the use of the
entire three floors was required; and a few years later a
large extension was added on 15th Street.

Departments and Workshops.

WITH the removal to Union
Square, many new departments
were added. While at 550–552
Broadway, Tiffany & Co. had gratuitously stored many valuables for their patrons; they now portioned off half of
the entire basement for a storage department with burglar-
proof vaults. Every facility was provided for the proper
care and protection of family silverware, jewels, heirlooms,
and valuables of every description. As with most of the
other departments, this one has since been twice enlarged.

The first floor was divided up between the silver, diamond, jewelry, watch, fancy-goods, leather-goods, umbrella,
stationery, plated-ware, watch-repairing, and jewelry and
silverware repairing departments, with offices in the rear;
while the entire second floor, with the exception of a portion
in the rear, reserved for the executive and bookkeepers'
offices, was devoted to the display of art works in bronzes,
statuary, bric-à-brac, clocks, mantel sets, lamps, curios, re-
productions of ancient armor, and ornamental objects for
home decoration.

TIFFANY & CO.'S NEW PLATED-WARE WORKS,
Forest Hill. Newark, N. J.

The limited stock at the old store of a few choice pieces of fancy porcelain and glassware was now enlarged to a special department for high-class pottery and cut glass. This collection occupies the third floor, and here everything in that line required for the proper furnishing of a household could be obtained, while special attention was given to securing choice specimens of antique glass and pottery, and examples of the most beautiful of modern products to be found in the European markets.

The two upper floors afforded ample facilities for organizing new shops and enlarging the old ones. These are located at present as follows: Third floor extension, Watch and Fan Shops; Fourth floor, Engraving and Art Department, Stationery, Printing and Stamping, Silver-polishing, and Clock Shops; Fifth floor, Jewelry, Diamond cutting and polishing, Case and Leather-work shops.

Since the removal to Union Square, the manufacture of electro-silver-plated ware has been added to the business. From a small shop in Newark, N. J., this branch of their manufactures has so expanded that a year ago a seven-acre plot was purchased at Forest Hill, a suburb of Newark, N. J., and the erection of a large plant begun, which has recently been completed; the new works at present occupy 45,000 square feet, and are so designed that additional wings and stories can be added to meet further requirements.

The many improvements in the processes of manufacturing, both in machinery and methods, the employment of larger forces of skilled mechanics, and other advantages possible with the increased facilities, will afford this department opportunities for further expansion which it has heretofore not enjoyed.

Review — 1867 = 1893. REVIEWING the results of the last quarter of a century's activity,—from the Paris Exposition of 1867 to 1893,—this era of peace and development shows a succession of international victories of great significance to American industries.

At the Centennial Exhibition in 1876, Tiffany & Co.'s exhibit of the masterpieces of their art in the various departments left them virtually without competitors. In addition to a gold medal, special recognition and certificates of award were bestowed for the display of jewelry, jeweled watches, silverware, silver inlaid with niello and copper, and wedding stationery.

The recognition and awards which Tiffany & Co. received at the Paris Exposition of 1867 have already been mentioned, and the honors bestowed upon them at the last two Universal Expositions held at Paris in 1878 and 1889 are of too recent date to call for any comment. In 1878 they received the *Grand Prix* for silverware, a gold medal for jewelry, and six medals to colaborers; while Mr. Tiffany, who attended the Exposition, was made the recipient of distinguished honors. He was created a Chevalier of the National Legion of Honor of France, and from the Emperor of Russia he received the Gold Medal *Præmia Digno*—an exceptional tribute. Then followed appointments as Imperial and Royal Jewelers, Gold and Silversmiths to most of the monarchs and dignitaries of Europe.

At the Exposition of 1889 the *Grand Prix* for silverware was again awarded to the house. Mr. E. C. Moore, the late manager of the works, was created a Chevalier and decorated with the ribbon of the Legion of Honor. In addition to this, sixteen other medals were awarded to the productions of the house: gold medals respectively for jewelry, precious stones of North America, leather-work, ivory carved and mounted, copperplate engraving and printing; silver and bronze medals respectively for glassware and clocks; and ten medals to colaborers.

3A

THE TIFFANY PAVILION,
World's Columbian Exposition.

Columbian Exposition. The exhibit made by Tiffany & Co. at the World's Columbian Exposition of 1893 is of too recent occurrence to comment upon at length. The testimonials, however, from the thousands of daily visitors, the almost unlimited generous comments of the press, and the valued technical reviews by art writers at home and abroad, have all been so overwhelming that the house accepts them not in the spirit of a personal compliment, but as a graceful tribute to the development of art metal-work in this country. The views and opinion of so eminent an authority as the London "Art Journal" are of interest in this connection. After reviewing the Tiffany Exhibit, the writer says in the October number:

"Passing to the exhibit of Messrs. Tiffany & Co., of New York, one finds a display more varied in expression and original in design, more distinctive and individual, than the work of any other firm in the Art metal group. And above all we must note the distinctively American characteristics of many of the exhibits here.

"Judging by the productions exhibited, one may well be in doubt whether our much-boasted European preëminence in these things is to last much longer, and whether, after all, we shall not in the near future be compelled to regard the firms of New York as at least our equals, if not our superiors, in the production of high-class gold and silver work."

Up to the hour of going to press Tiffany & Co. have received fifty-five awards at the World's Columbian Exposition; but while these many additional honors are appreciated, they mean but little compared with that calm verdict of public approval so generously given. It is this compliment for which Tiffany & Co. are grateful, and their feeling of appreciation finds constant expression in their aim to excel the past, and to retain by real merit the approval of the public.

War Testimonials.
THE products of Tiffany & Co.'s workshops that could be classed under this heading are so numerous that only those associated with historic incidents or of general interest are mentioned below:

General Schuyler Hamilton, U. S. A. Sword presented by his fellow-citizens of New-York in recognition of his services in the Mexican War, 1848.

Dr. E. K. Kane and Commander H. S. Hartstein, Arctic explorers, 1858. Gold medals presented by the State of New-York in recognition of their services to the world in Arctic discoveries, and their gallant search for Sir John Franklin. The medals cost $1000 and $500 respectively, the former weighing 14 ounces, and the latter 6 ounces, of pure gold.

Before the close of the war, and for some time after, the facilities of Tiffany & Co. were taxed to their utmost with orders for testimonials of every description for presentation to the heroes of the battle-fields; hundreds of richly mounted testimonial swords were made, many of them set with precious stones and costing from $500 to $10,000.

Perhaps the most notable of these was the sword presented by Tiffany & Co. to the great Sanitary Fair held in New-York City in 1864, and voted to General U. S. Grant. The scabbard was of gold, and richly studded with rubies, diamonds, and sapphires, representing the national colors.

General G. B. McClellan was a close competitor. The votes were sold at $1.00 each, and the sword realized nearly $100,000.

Among other presentation swords and testimonials of note made by Tiffany & Co., were the following:

Sword presented to General W. T. Sherman after the Battle of Shiloh, 1862.

Sword presented to General J. C. Frémont, the "Pathfinder of the West," 1862.

Sword presented to Major-General H. W. Halleck by the ladies of St. Louis, 1862.

Sword presented to Major-General Ambrose E. Burnside by the State of Rhode Island, 1862.

Sword presented to Brigadier-General J. J. Stevens by the non-commissioned officers and privates of the 79th Highland Guard, N. Y. S. M., at Beaufort, S. C., 1862.

Sword presented to Colonel Rush C. Hawkins, of the Hawkins Zouaves, by his fellow-citizens of New-York, 1863.

Sword presented to Captain Percival Drayton, U. S. N., by his fellow-citizens of New-York, 1863.

Sword presented to Brigadier-General T. E. G. Ransom by the officers of his brigade, 1863.

Sword presented to Admiral David G. Farragut, U. S. N., by his friends in the Union League Club of New-York, 1864.

Set of silver tankard pitchers and goblets, eleven pieces, presented to Colonel Abram Duryee, 7th Regiment, by the merchants of New-York, 1860.

Trumpet presented to Captain H. H. Eldridge, of the steamer "Atlantic," by the 3d New Hampshire Volunteers at Port Royal, 1862.

Medals struck to commemorate the battle of the "Monitor" and the "Merrimac," 1862.

Medal presented to General George H. Thomas by the State of Tennessee, 1865. It bore his famous words, "I will hold the town till we starve."

Inkstand presented to President Abraham Lincoln by Charles D. Poston, Esq., 1865.

Other Presentation Pieces.

MARRIAGE of General Tom Thumb and Lavinia Warren at Grace Church, New-York, February 10, 1863. Silver chariot presented by Tiffany & Co.

Atlantic Cable completion. Testimonials presented to Cyrus W. Field, 1866:

Gold medal presented by the Government.

Gold box presented by Mayor Tillman, 1858.

Silver Epergne presented by the Directors of the New-York, Newfoundland, and London Telegraph Company, 1873.

Thomas Nast, Esq. Silver vase presented by members of the Union League Club, New-York, 1869.

Arbitrators of the "Alabama" Claims, 1873, — Count Frederic Sclopis, Viscomte A'Itajuba, Mr. J. Stæmpfli. Silver services presented by the United States Government, each set consisting of centerpiece, two jardinières, and a pair of candelabra.

Survivors of the "Ville du Havre" disaster, November 22, 1873. Silver tea-service presented by them to Captain Urquhart, of the "Trimountain," who rescued them from the sinking "Loch Earn."

Bryant Vase, 1876. Silver testimonial presented to William Cullen Bryant by his friends in commemoration of his eightieth birthday. [This vase, which was designed by Mr. James H. Whitehouse, and selected after an open competition, was universally pronounced to be the most artistic and notable production of our time.]

August Bartholdi, 1886. Silver Centerpiece, "Liberty Enlightening the World," testimonial from 121,000 Americans, through the New-York "World."

Charleston, S. C., 1887. Memorial Tablet presented by the City of Charleston to the Executive Relief Committee for unparalleled services after the earthquake of 1886.

William Ewart Gladstone. Silver Centerpiece testimonial from American admirers in recognition of his efforts to secure Home Rule for Ireland, 1887.

Sword presented to General Nelson A. Miles by the people of Arizona, 1887.

The yachting trophies made for most of the International and Annual Yacht Club regattas held within forty years, numerous rifle prizes, pigeon-shooting cups, racing cups, and prizes of every description, cannot be enumerated here. A few of the most recent of the above were shown in the Loan Collection of Tiffany & Co.'s exhibit at the World's Columbian Exposition, Chicago, 1893.

Appointments to Royal Courts, etc.

MESSRS. TIFFANY & CO. have been appointed Imperial and Royal Jewelers, Gold and Silversmiths to the following monarchs and dignitaries of Europe:

Her Most Gracious Majesty The Queen of England.
His Royal Highness The Prince of Wales.
Her Royal Highness The Princess of Wales.
His Royal Highness The Duke of Edinburgh.
His Imperial Majesty The Emperor of Russia.
Her Imperial Majesty The Empress of Russia.
His Imperial Highness The Grand Duke Vladimir.
His Royal Highness The Grand Duke Alexis.
His Imperial Highness The Grand Duke Paul.
His Royal Highness The Grand Duke Sergius.
His Imperial Majesty The Emperor of Austria.
His Majesty The King of Prussia.
His Majesty The King of the Belgians.
His Majesty The King of Italy.
His Majesty The King of Denmark.
His Majesty The King of Greece.
His Majesty The King of Spain.
His Majesty The King of Portugal.
His Majesty The King of Roumania.

His Imperial Majesty The Emperor of Brazil.
His Majesty The Khedive of Egypt.
His Imperial Majesty The Shah of Persia.
Her Royal Highness The Infanta Doña Eulalia.

Mr. Tiffany's Personality. THE story of the house of Tiffany & Co. has been briefly told, and the life of Charles L. Tiffany dwelt upon as identified with the business which he founded. His name is inseparably associated with every stage of the development of the house. But he has always frankly recognized and commended the services of his associates and colaborers, and he never speaks of his business career without feelingly referring to all those whose indefatigable labors in the various branches of the business and departments of its manufactures have contributed so much to Tiffany & Co.'s success. A sense of delicacy, however, forbids much that might be said touching his personality—the qualities that command the respect of the community and the good will of the world—that make lifelong friends of acquaintances—and retain employees from the end of their school-days to the end of their lives.

This side of Mr. Tiffany's life is yet to be told, and that the time may yet be far distant is the sincere wish of the thousand and more in his employ, his hundreds of friends scattered throughout the land, and the many thousands more who know him only by his deeds.

As a representative business man Mr. Tiffany has been honored with many positions of trust in the metropolis, and few philanthropic or other public movements have originated in the city without his aid and support. He is a liberal patron of Art, and in its advancement in America has shown the keenest interest.

Among the public institutions, societies, and other associations with which Mr. Tiffany is identified are the following:

A Founder of the New-York Society of Fine Arts.

A Founder of the Union League Club of New-York.

Trustee of the Metropolitan Museum of Art.

A Founder of the Restigouche Salmon Club of Matapedia, Canada.

Trustee of the American Museum of Natural History.

Fellow of the Geographical Society.

Fellow of the National Academy of Design.

Director of the Bank of the Metropolis.

Director of the Pacific Bank.

Director of the American Surety Co.

Director of the State Trust Co.

Member of the New-York Historical Society.

Member of the American Protective Tariff League.

Member of the Chamber of Commerce.

Member of the Union Club.

Member of the New-York Club.

Member of the New-York Jockey Club.

Member of the South Side Sportsmen's Club of Long Island.

Member of the West Island Club of Rhode Island.

Member of the Young Men's Christian Association; and a life-member of many charitable and philanthropic organizations.

Directors.

The directors of the house of Tiffany & Co. at present are:
CHARLES L. TIFFANY, *President and Treasurer.*
CHARLES T. COOK, *Vice-President and Assistant Treasurer.*
PAULDING FARNHAM, *Secretary.*

Trustees:

CHARLES L. TIFFANY.   CHARLES T. COOK.
LOUIS C. TIFFANY.   PAULDING FARNHAM.
JOHN C. MOORE.   ALFRED MITCHELL.

Manager of the Paris Branch:
CHARLES M. MOORE.